Michelle Barnette

Love Me Now

Salamander Street

PLAYS

First published in 2021 by Salamander Street Ltd.
(info@salamanderstreet.com)

ISBN: 9781913630881

Cover artwork by Rebecca Pitt

Printed and bound in Great Britain

10 9 8 7 6 5 4 3 2 1

ACKNOWLEDGEMENTS

It is a unique privilege to write acknowledgements nearly three years after *Love Me Now* first opened. Anyone who works in theatre knows that a production's success is due to the hard work of many, not the inspiration of one. And hard work has never been as much fun as it was collaborating with this extraordinary group of people.

A special thank you to Jamie Armitage, whose unwavering belief and support made me, and the play, better for it. It is no small task to find someone who loves a play you write in all its messy early drafts and sees its potential, who nudges and guides its development with a light hand and who isn't afraid to challenge the things you've left in because you love them even though they no longer make sense by the fifth draft. I could not have asked for a better friend, confidante and collaborator through this process. Thank you.

To Helena, Ali and Bruno, who stuck with me even as I rewrote the final scene three days before tech, who worked so beautifully together and who made this play such an utter joy to watch. My hat goes off to you all, for your work then and for all of the amazing things you've done since. Thank you for bringing it to life.

To the brilliant production team – Fin, SJP, Andy, Ben, Rachel, Enric, Alex, Chloé and William. I couldn't have wished for a better team and I am so very grateful for your ongoing love, friendship and the joy of – even now – getting to continuously bask in your talent.

To Joel Fisher, who no longer works in theatre but who was a steady friend and champion of *Love Me Now*.

To the team at the Actors Centre, who were so supportive throughout the original run.

To Arun Blair-Mangat, Cameron Cuffe, David Witts, Ed Hayter, James Northcote, Alexander Forsyth and Sara Joyce who were a part of the early development process.

To George Spender and Salamander Street for their care and support in giving *Love Me Now* a life in print, letting B's story live again.

To my mom, Jenny, my inspiration and best friend. My dad and brother, Mark and Michael, for their unwavering love and support.

To my partner, Chris Harding, who I hadn't met when *Love Me Now* was on. I am exceptionally grateful that you are nothing like any of the characters in this play.

To everyone who, advertently or inadvertently, contributed to bringing this play to life whether that be through conversations down the pub, introducing me to members of the team, putting up with my incessant talking about the show, or simply coming to watch it.

And finally, to all those who love me now.

I have resisted the urge to edit the play with a new eye and so I present it now as it was when it was last performed.

Michelle Barnette, January 2021

For anyone who has ever been B

Love Me Now was first performed at the Tristan Bates Theatre in London as a co-production with the Actors Centre on 27 March 2018.

The cast *(in order of speaking)* was as follows:

A   Alistair Toovey

B   Helena Wilson

C   Gianbruno Spena

Director	Jamie Armitage
Set & Costume Designer	Fin Redshaw
Lighting Designer	Ben Jacobs
Sound Designer	Andrew Josephs
Casting Director	Sarah-Jane Price
Fight and Intimacy Director	Enric Ortuño
Stage Manager	Rachel Pryce
Production Manager	William Nelson
Artwork	Rebecca Pitt
PR	Alex Shaw for Chloé Nelkin Consulting

– indicates an interrupted thought

Text in *( )* that follows a – should be vocalized but the sentence does not need to be finished

/ indicates where the text should overlap

Text is columns should be read as laid out

Character List

A: Male, early-mid twenties. Should know better.

B: Female, early-mid twenties. Searching.

C: Male, mid-late twenties. More put together than the other two.

SCENE 1

One year ago

A *and* **B** *are lying in bed – they have clearly just finished having sex. There is no physical contact between the two.*

A: Wow.

B: You can say that again.

A: Wow...

B: Lost for words?

A: Perhaps.

B: An improvement?

A: Quite.

B: I took up yoga – supposed to be good for my core. Flexibility and all that nonsense. Could you tell?

A: Mmm…

B: It's great.

A: Yeah.

B: I mean, I only go twice a week but there was this study that said that thinking of doing exercise was as effective as actually *doing* the exercise.

A: That's not exactly how the gym works –

B: I'll send you the link.

A: It's fine.

B: It isn't a problem –

A: – really. I believe you.

B: It'll take two seconds.

B *finds her phone and sends him the link. His phone beeps.*

B: Now you can read it on your way home.

A: Thanks.

B: Tell me what you think.

A: Sure.

B: It's amazing though – just going to yoga once a week and you noticed the difference.

A: Twice, you – *(said)*

B: – and most of that was just me *thinking* of doing yoga, so really it was only like, half a session a week –

A: – how do you do *half* a session / of yoga?

B: / I mean really I never *actually* went to yoga.

A: You said you took it up. 'Took it up' implies attendance.

B: Well I invested in it. I bought a mat and everything.

A: You bought a mat.

B: Yeah.

A: Do you use it?

B: Well, no –

A: – well that's not yoga.

B: You don't need a mat to do yoga.

A: Oh my god.

B: Every time I put on the outfit I just don't feel in the yoga kind of mood –

A: – surely that – *(defeats the purpose)*

B: Sure, the outfits look cute when you buy them – but then you actually put them on and it's like you suffocate. I think they've done it on purpose, you know. The fitness industry. They invented camel toe so you'd hate yourself so much you'd exercise until you lose it. Like it's motivation or something. But I want to do is put my trackies back on and get the Ben and Jerry's.

An awkward silence.

B: So I really seemed more flexible?

A: No.

B: But you said –

A: I murmured.

B: A murmur of approval.

A: Not quite.

B: *(Imitating.)* Mmmm....

A: I was being nice.

B: Oh.

A: It's fine, really –

B: Well maybe that wasn't the best position to demonstrate with –

A: – it was fine –

B: – let me show you what we were doing / in class

A: / you don't go to class –

B: – in the Youtube videos –

A: That is not going to class –

B: – let me just show you / what they were doing

A: / there's really no need –

B: You'll love this / it's called the downward dog

B *demonstrates.*

A: / really, that's more than enough –

B: Best view in the house, lucky you…

B *gets up and goes to kiss* **A**. *A breaks free, gets up and begins to recover articles of clothing. During this scene* **B** *may attempt to remove* **A**'s *clothing as he puts it on.*

A: Right, well I best be off.

B: We have time for one more go –

A: Next time.

B: You always say – *(that)*

A: – I forgot I have a drinks thing. Next time.

B: Next time.

A: Promise.

B *roams her hand around to* **A***'s crotch, he lets her.* **B** *gives* **A** *a blowjob.*

SCENE 2

Two and a half years ago

A *and* **B** *have just finished having sex. Something has made them laugh. They are laughing uncontrollably. They calm down. Silence.*

A: So.

B: So

A: Now what?

B: We can sit.

A: In silence?

B: Yeah.

A: That's awkward.

B: Only if you make it awkward.

A: True.

Silence.

A: How's your family?

B: Fine.

A: Your dog?

B: Getting old. Cute as ever.

A: Nice.

B: Yeah.

A: Water?

B: No. Thanks.

SCENE 3

One year ago

B *has just finished the blowjob.* **A** *gets sorted and begins to head for the door.*

A: Cheers babe.

B: That's it?

A: I wasn't aware that was in the yoga curriculum.

B: You've got to be kidding me.

A: I don't have time for this.

B: You're just going to go, now?

A: Yes.

B: You never stay.

A: Don't try to make this into something it's not.

B: I just gave you head!

A: I didn't ask for it /

B: / I didn't hear you complaining –

A: – and had you asked I would've said no / rather firmly

B: / Excuse me? /

A: / Technically that would qualify as rape –

B: You can't cry rape / if you encouraged it!

A: / But you were so keen I figured I'd give you the practice –

B: – oh for fuck's sake –

A: You could certainly do with it.

This hits **B** *like a slap in the face.*

B: So it's not enough that I was gagging –

A: – Oh, not now –

B: – because gagging is just part of the job description right? You think you've come in here and done me some huge fucking favour, letting me suck your cock –

A: – there are people who would pay to suck my cock. Consider yourself lucky you got it for free.

B: You're such an ass.

A: You love it.

B: Hardly.

A: Oh come on, I'm teasing.

B: Ha ha.

A: You got plans tonight?

B: Just going for a drink. You're welcome to come.

A: Can't.

B: Fine.

A: Anyway.

B: Anyway.

A: See you later.

B: You know, just gimme a sec to get ready –

A: – I've got to go –

B: – two seconds, I'll get the tube with you.

A: Fine.

She gets ready casually.

B: So what are you doing tonight then?

A: You know. Seeing a man about a dog.

B: What are you actually doing?

A: Drinks.

B: Oh.

It's taking too long.

A: I've really got to – *(go)*

B: Sorry, sorry, nearly there.

She finishes up, she's not going anywhere special. She gets her stuff, goes to the door. The door doesn't budge.

B: Oh fucks sake.

A: Everything okay?

B: It's stuck.

A: Let me try.

It doesn't work. Tries to shove the door open. Nothing. **A** *tries again.* **A** *needn't have bothered – the door isn't going anywhere.*

A: Fucking fuck. Now what?

B: There's a window.

A: We're on the seventh floor.

B: And?

A: I'm not jumping out of a fucking window.

B: It happens sometimes.

A: Suicide?

B: The door.

A: How convenient.

B: And suicide.

A: Is there someone you can call?

B: I'll text the landlord.

A: What, you afraid of actually having to string together a sentence on the spot?

B: Fine. *(B calls – no answer.)* Happy?

A: Leave a voicemail.

B: He's more likely to read a text.

A: Fine.

She sends a text.

A: Have you got any tools?

B: Tools?

A: I can fix the door.

B: Do I seem like the kind of person who has tools?

A: Guess not.

Silence.

A: Can we have a drink at least?

B: Tap water, tea, tequila –

A: – tequila.

B: No lemons.

A: Fuck the lemons. Pass the bottle.

She does. He drinks from the bottle.

B: But your drinks –

A: I am drinking.

Silence

B: Give it here.

He does. She drinks.

Silence.

A: How many yoga outfits did you buy?

B: Four.

A: Four?

B: …teen.

A: Even yogis don't have fourteen outfits –

B: – no point doing something if you don't look good doing it.

A: Surely the whole point of yoga is to live a holistic life.

B: Or you do it for the Instagram picture.

A: Oh yeah, sorry.

Silence.

A: How fucking shallow.

B: Sorry?

A: Yoga. Doing it for the Instagram photo.

B: Oh fuck off.

A: But people do it.

B: And?

A: Pathetic. Why learn yoga to impress someone else?

B: I need more booze.

A: It is though.

B: Are you always so cynical?

A: Honest babe, the word is honest.

B: Well, can you be honest silently?

Silence.

A: Shall we do some yoga then?

B: Oh my god –

A: You can show me your cats cradle…

B: That's not a yoga move.

A: How would you know?

B: I just do.

A: Then you also know they're called yoga 'poses' right?

B: Obviously.

A: Just checking.

Silence.

A: Shall we?

B: No.

A: One pose.

B: You're just going to be a dick about it –

A: No, no I promise. Please. I want to learn.

B: If you start laughing…

A: I won't.

They do yoga very seriously (not at all). **A** *laughs.*

B: You're the actual worst.

A: You love it.

Silence.

A: What's this called?

B: Not sure.

Silence

B: Will you take a picture of me?

A: Absolutely not –

B: – oh, come on –

A: This. This is why you need a boyfriend.

B: Oh yeah?

A: Yeah. That's what they're for.

B: Know anyone?

A: Ha.

They resume 'yoga'.

A: When was your last relationship?

B: You know the answer.

A: Go on…

B: Please not now.

A: Why are you single?

B: This is really killing my zen.

A: You're not zen.

B: I'm like the definition of zen.

A: But –

B: Don't break my flow.

A: Why are you single?

B: And breathe out…

A: It's nothing to be ashamed of! You're young. You won't die alone.
    Probably.

B: Oh thanks –

A: – no seriously. You're not that bad.

B: Glowing review, that.

A: Come on. Why are you single?

B: I don't know, ask my exes.

A: I'm asking you.

B: You'd probably know the answer better than I do.

A: I do know the answer.

B: Then why ask?

A: Because it's fun.

B: Go on then, Sherlock. Enlighten me.

A: You're too picky. And too hung up on idiots like me.

B: Ha.

A: Nail on the head?

B: Or men just don't want to hang around when they roll over and realize what they've gotten themselves into. Literally.

A: Would you like some balloons for your pity party?

B: If you don't like my answer don't bother asking.

A: Seriously – where's this crap coming from?

B: Excuse me?

A: You're usually alright in bed, you don't smell and you don't pretend that the intake of a single carbohydrate will cause you to spontaneously combust. Three ticks if you ask me.

B: Charming.

A: So really behind this thoroughly passable exterior you're crippled by insecurity.

B: Sounds like you know a lot about it.

A: I can read you like a book.

B: I meant your crippling insecurity.

A: Oh?

B: Yeah. In psychology they call that projection.

A: You're the one going on and on about how you pig out on Ben and Jerry's and hate the camel toe it gives you –

B: – the lady doth project too much, methinks.

A: Hardly.

B: I'm not a damsel in distress.

A: No. Just a coward.

SCENE 4

Two years ago

A *&* **B** *are about to have sex.* **B** *stops.*

B: You never told me why you stopped seeing that last girl.

A: She was a bitch.

B: Oh?

Kissing continues.

A: Emphasis on the 'itch.'

B: Oh.

A: Don't worry, I'm clean.

B: Have you been tested?

A: No.

B: How can you know you're clean if you've never been tested?

A: I use condoms.

More kissing.

B: Condoms don't always work.

A: They do the job.

B: But do they?

A: Yes.

B: What if someone had a cold sore?

A: Do you have a cold sore?

B: No of course not –

A: Well why would someone else have a cold sore?

B: Because they're so common. The statistic is that like 90% of people have them –

A: – no more statistics, come on. Kiss me.

B *kisses him. Her heart isn't in it.* **A** *stops.*

A: Seriously?

B: I just can't get it out of my head.

A: We've had sex and you're still clean, right?

B: Well yeah –

A: So it's fine. Come on…

B: How many people are you sleeping with right now?

A: Five.

B: Five?

A: It's not a big deal.

B: When did that happen?

A: Since I last saw you.

B: Oh my god –

A: You're sleeping with other people too.

B: Do they know?

A: No.

B: Fucking hell.

A: Anyway, it doesn't matter. I do a spot check.

B: Sorry?

A: Eyes: not bloodshot. Check. Nose: not running. Check. Lips, are you about to give me herpes? No? Check. Vagina: Don't see any crabs. Check.

B: Penis, discolored? Check. Leave them with blue balls? Check.

A: See, you get it. Now…

B: You are a walking STD risk.

A: Don't be like this –

B: What if you got herpes from one of them?

A: Stop being paranoid.

B: I'm not being paranoid, I'm being safe.

A: What's wrong?

B: Nothing's wrong.

A: Something's wrong and it isn't my dick. Are you going to tell me?

B: I'm fine.

A: Fine. *(Beat.)* I'm gonna get going.

B: I didn't realize there were others.

A: We've never been exclusive.

B: But five? Plus me? I know you haven't done anything wrong, I just feel a bit…

A: Disposable?

B: Dirty.

A: Ah.

B: Disposable?

A: You should be happy.

B: Oh?

A: Yeah. Five women and I'm still here choosing to fuck you.

B: Charming.

A: When was the last time you slept with someone else?

B: Oh fuck off.

A: Come on, tell me.

B: None of your business.

A: I know there was that last guy –

B: Which one?

A: There she is.

A kisses her forcefully. **B** *is not into it but goes along with it anyway.*

SCENE 5

One year ago

A: *(Affronted.)* I'm not a coward.

B: Right.

A: I'm not!

B: Then why are you so terrified of commitment?

A: That's not cowardly, that's smart.

B: Oh?

A: Yeah. No commitment, no one else to think about. You just pick up and go.

B: Must be lonely.

A: You're breaking the rules.

B: We don't have any rules.

A: No serious chats.

B: We never have serious chats –

A: This? Becoming a serious chat.

B: We are fully capable of having conversations like normal human beings –

A: What are we meant to do until your landlord shows?

B: Talk. We can talk.

A: About what?

B: Anything.

A: I don't want to.

B: Has anyone told you how annoying you are?

A: Just you.

B: I doubt that.

A: But –

B: Sit. Chill. I won't bite. We already know you're not into that…

A: Hilarious.

B: We could – *(have sex)*

A: – not again.

B: Right.

A: Ah fucking hell. Where's the landlord?!

B: I don't know.

A: This is fucking with my night.

B: What did you have on?

A: A date.

B: Oh.

A: Thought I'd be able to lock it in –

B: – not planning on a shower?

A: I was going to go home first.

B: That's grim.

A: She'd never know.

B: I guess.

A: Could I shower here?

B: Fuck off.

A: Fair.

Silence.

B: So who's the new girl?

A: A girl.

B: How'd you meet?

A: Tinder.

B: Oh.

A: She's fucking great –

B: Fucking great or great fucking?

A: To be determined.

B: Have you met her yet?

A: Yeah, second date.

B: What's she like?

A: Blonde, blue eyed, great ass –

B: – but what's she like?

A: She's fine.

B: Oh.

A: You know I love my blondes.

B: I've got a date tomorrow.

A: I've got one now.

B: New guy. Has his PhD in applied mathematics.

A: Right.

B: I thought you didn't want a relationship.

A: Being with Fiona wouldn't be the worst thing in the world.

B: Fiona. Pretty name.

A: Yeah.

B: So not the worst thing in the world.

A: No.

B: Why?

A: Why not?

B: You don't want a relationship.

A: Well you haven't seen Fiona yet –

B: Is that all it is to you? Looks?

A: Well no –

B: Well then, why not me?

A: Sorry?

B: Why am I not good enough for you?

Silence.

B: I asked a question.

Silence.

A: It isn't that.

B: What then?

A: Don't make this weird.

B: We can't keep doing this.

A: I know.

B: I need to know.

A: You won't like the answer.

B: Well you don't get to decide that for me –

A: – stop embarrassing yourself –

B: – and I want to know

SCENE 6

B *has been talking about this major project at work. This has been going on for a while –*

B: The campaign went off without a hitch. The MD pulled me aside after the meeting to tell me how happy he was with the work/ and –

A: / That's brilliant /

B: / Thanks – and he asked me to head the major pitch we have for a really important client / it's my first time –

A: / Well done!

B: / Do you mind?

A: What?

B: Stop interrupting me.

A: Oh. Sorry.

B: So yeah. My first time heading my own team.

A: Heading?

B: Yeah, like taking on the project and picking the –

A: No no, the other head.

B: Oh my god.

A: Fancy it?

B: You are so lame.

A: Come on, it'll be fun.

B: You're horny now?

A: Well, we're here. We've spent ages talking. We like sex.

B: We agreed last time that we're not having sex anymore.

A: We've agreed that before.

31

B: In fact I believe it was you who made me promise that we'd never have sex again –

A: Well I obviously wasn't being serious.

B: Tough luck.

A: It'll be fun.

B: Have you seen the movie Teeth?

A: What?

B: The one where her vagina has teeth inside so if you do something even vaguely non-consensual it'll bite your penis off.

A: …

B: No? I figured that would put you off.

A: Where do you come up with this shit?

B: No.

A: For old time's sake.

B: You say it like it's been years.

A: It feels like it!

B: It's been a couple of months. You'll live. Anyway, so it looks like there may be a big promotion coming up, if I nail – *(the next pitch)*

A: Please?

B: No.

A: Just sex.

B: Sorry?

A: You don't even have to go down on me. In, out, down. It'll be over in like, two minutes.

B: Tempting.

A: So that's a yes?

B: No, that's called sarcasm.

A: Oh come on –

B: Sarcasm is this thing where you say one thing and –

A: I know what sarcasm is.

B: Phew.

A: Why not?

B: Believe it or not, 'in and out' sex isn't exactly appealing.

A: Head then.

B: Oh my god.

A: I know how much you love it.

B: You're relentless.

A: It'll be great.

B: No.

A: Do I have to beg?

B: You're doing a pretty good job of that already –

A: One blowjob for the road. Please.

B: What are you willing to do for it?

A: Want me to get on my knees? I will. I'll do it.

B: Don't be ridiculous –

A: I'm not kidding. Say the word. I'll do it.

B: Go on then.

A *gets on his knees.*

A: I'm begging you.

B: Begging me for what?

A: A blowjob.

B: Get up –

A: Nope. Not until you say yes.

B: This is ridiculous. Get up.

A: I'm not moving.

B *gets on her knees.*

B: I'm not having sex with you.

A: Oral sex?

B: Oral sex is sex. We're not having sex.

A: I'll do you first.

B: Get up –

A: How about we leave this to fate?

B: What?

A: A coin.

B: We don't need a coin when I've already told you no.

A: But you love head.

B: I love head, but I don't love you ignoring me for two weeks afterwards.

A: I won't do that.

B: You will.

A: I promise.

B: You always do.

A: Let's flip a coin.

B: We're not –

A: – let fate decide. Heads we have head.

Silence.

B: You're a ridiculous human being

A: Is that a yes?

B: I can't believe you.

A: You still haven't said no…

SCENE 7

One year ago

B: You might as well tell me.

A: No.

B: I'm going to assume the worst anyway.

A: Go on then.

B: Maybe it's that I like sex too much. Or I'm too flippant? Or too intelligent – I get that one a lot – or too intense.

A: Stop it –

B: – Or perhaps it's that I'm the only person who actually understands you and that fucking terrifies you because you can't fucking hide with me –

A: Enough.

B: Or –

A: I said enough. I'm not going to watch you humiliate yourself.

Silence.

B: I just can't.

A: I'm not going to tell you.

B: I mean us.

A: Right.

B: I mean it this time.

A: So, see you next month yeah?

B: No.

A: Oh get off it. You say this every time. Then you shag someone else and when he dumps you you come crawling back / to fuck me –

B: / Fuck you.

A: My charm is overwhelming.

B: Something is

A: Lighten up –

B: No. Fuck off. You call me.

A: Well, you let me.

B: It's just not going to happen / this time

A: / just go fuck that ex of yours –

B: – what ex? –

A: The one you ran to last time –

B: You don't know what you're talking about.

A: Don't I?

B: No.

A: Oh come on – you and me, we're apples from the same tree.

B: I'm nothing like you.

A: Oh go on then, how many men have you shagged?

B: Ever?

A: Recently.

B: Define recent.

A: This year.

B: Doesn't matter.

A: There was the army officer, the web designer, the stoner, the guy who wanted to be a priest, the / one who had a kid…

B: / You don't know what you're talking about.

A: You didn't date them?

B: I didn't sleep with them.

A: Go on then. How many?

B: One.

Silence.

A: One. *(Beat.)* I don't believe you.

B: Believe it.

A: You dirty fucking liar.

B: Don't speak to me that way –

A: You pretend you're all sexually fucking liberal and you sleep around and you don't care and you suddenly fucking tell me that you've been leading me on this whole / fucking time?!

B: / leading *you* on?!

A: Leading me on! The fuck are you doing, only sleeping with me? How fucking pathetic. I don't believe you –

B: – there's nothing to believe –

A: – you're just trying to make me feel guilty. Guess what? Not going to fucking happen –

B: Great. Good, fine. Just enough –

A: I –

B: ENOUGH

A: I can't believe it. You should've slept around.

B: Why?

A: Because we meant nothing to each other.

B: That's not true.

A: Yes it is.

B: Of course it isn't –

A: This is exactly what we said it was – sex.

B: That isn't what you said it was.

A: Yes –

B: – No. No, you told me this could be whatever I wanted it to be.

A: I've got to use that line again.

B: You're ridiculous.

A: And what do you want it to be?

B: Now?

A: Yes.

B: Nothing.

A: Nothing.

B: Yeah.

A: Good.

B: Good.

A: You know, if you had an ounce of self respect you would never let anyone treat you the way I've treated you.

B: Why do you do it?

A: Why not?

B: If your mother saw –

A: – leave my mum out of it –

B: – She'd be so disappointed.

A: Well she'll never know, will she?

B: I could tell her.

A: You wouldn't dare.

B: Wouldn't I? She knows me. She thinks I'm great.

A: That should never have happened.

B: Well you shouldn't have invited me over then –

A: I didn't think she'd show up –

B: – You had already told her about me.

A: That was a mistake.

B: What would she say, do you think? About how badly you've treated me?

A: Fuck off.

B: Would she ever be able to look you in the eyes again, do you think? Probably not, you know. You'd just be just another asshole who screws over women –

A: Don't.

B: Because that's what you are. Just another asshole.

A: I suggest you stop.

B: Why? It's the truth, isn't it? Can you imagine… what if, what if someone did this to her? Before she had you? How would you feel?

A: This isn't some Freudian shit.

B: What would you do? Punch him? Beat the guy?

A: I've never hurt anyone.

B: Oh?

A: Not physically.

B: Right.

A: Fuck off –

B: I seem to have struck a nerve.

A: And what would your father say, huh? If he saw the little slut he's raised? You think he'd be so fucking proud of you?

B: Don't bring my dad into this.

A: What, you can give but you can't take?

B: You know that isn't fair.

A: Isn't it?

B: You know very well it isn't.

A: It's probably why he left, you know. Couldn't bear to see what a fucking disgrace you'd become. Didn't want to hang around to watch you self destruct.

B: You know what, you're probably right. I'm just going to be alone for the rest of my life, huh. Because I'm not worth anything.

A: Stop it –

B: – stop what? You're right. I'm just another whore as far as you're concerned. So fuck off and leave me alone.

A: I didn't mean it.

B: Yes you did.

A: I'm sorry.

B: No you're not. This is all because of you. You did this. You know that, right?

A: You expect me to buy that?

B: I was a different person before you. I'm done. No more sex. No more treating me badly.

A: That's for the best.

B: And you're never to bring up my father again.

A: Then keep my mum out of it.

SCENE 8

One year and three months ago

A *and* **B** *have been taking great pleasure in teasing each other.* **A** *prepares to leave.*

A: You're an idiot.

B: Seriously –

A: So easily wound up.

B: Says you.

A: Yeah.

B: Takes one to know one.

A: Great comeback.

B: I don't need a comeback when I have the truth.

A: Which is?

She has no idea where she was going with this.

B: Well since we're not sleeping together anymore I guess I can tell you.

A: Hm?

B: You were never that great in bed.

A: You told me I was the best sex you'd ever had.

B: A year ago.

A: And you kept sleeping with me.

B: I've had a lot of sex since then.

A: Show off.

B: Learned a lot.

A: I'm great in bed.

B: Eh.

A: Don't 'eh' me!

B: Fair is fair.

A: Why was I bad?

B: Doesn't matter –

A: – you can't say that –

B: – oh yes I can.

A: Tease.

B: Jerk.

A: I'm not like this with everyone.

B: You know, you're right actually.

A: Can I get that in writing?

B: No no, I've seen you with your mum now. When we met the other week you literally held a fucking car door open for me –

A: – you were never meant to meet her –

B: – Well it happened.

A: But – *(I didn't plan it)*

B: – Do you know what my favorite part was though?

A: What?

B: You made me a cup of tea.

A: I always make you a cup of tea.

B: No you don't. I have to ask.

A: So?

B: I even timed it a couple times, normally it's two hours before –

A: We don't need to rehash this.

B: Don't we?

A: No. It's done. You should feel special really.

B: Special?

A: Yeah. I'm only like this with you.

B: Rude?

A: Only because you're clingy.

B: You're heartless.

A: You always want to know it all.

B: You're always having temper tantrums.

A: You need to learn to keep your mouth shut.

B: You would marry the gym if you could.

A: Saves me the future child support.

Somehow while this is going on, the two have gotten very close to one another.

B: You look silly in those baseball caps you wear.

A: You shouldn't wear crop tops.

B: Sometimes your feet smell.

A: Don't smell them.

B: I don't try to.

A: Sorry.

B: Are you?

A: Not at all.

They begin to kiss and grope. **B** *is not interested.*

A: What's wrong?

B: Nothing.

B *starts kissing* **A** *again.*

A: Do you want to do this?

B: Sure.

A: Because I don't think you want to do this.

B: It's fine. Look, I'm saying yes.

Without meaning to, she flinches as his hands begin to wander up her thighs.

A: You don't want to.

B: Shut up, will you?

*B carries on, but it's as if she is going through the motions. As **A** goes to remove **B**'s clothing, she flinches again.*

B: No. No I can't. I'm sorry.

A: Fuck's sake.

B: I'm sorry.

A: You can't just –

B: – I can. *(Beat.)* You should go.

A: I've been trying –

B: I know.

A: What then?

B: …

A: Tell me. What's going on?

B: I just. I can't.

A: Try.

B: I can't explain. I don't know. I just, don't want to.

A: You always want to.

B: I know –

A: I just never know –

B: – I know – *(I'm just trying to)*

A: Let me help. What's wrong?

B: Please, just go.

A: Fine.

B: Next time I'll – *(make it up to you)*

A: Is there a next time?

Silence.

SCENE 9

One year ago

A: The landlord should be here by now.

They drink.

A: You know, if this place were bigger it would be almost perfect.

B: Yeah?

A: Yeah.

B: That's probably the nicest thing you've ever said to me.

A: That's not true.

B: No?

A: I've said loads of nice things –

B: – like? –

A: – when you're not around.

B: Ah.

A: It'd go to your head otherwise.

B: What do you say?

A: About?

B: Me.

A: The usual stuff.

B: Go on.

A: You know. Normal stuff. Like how your place is almost perfect.

B: You're the worst.

A: You really want to know?

B: Obviously.

A: Um. That you're good at your job. That you aren't entirely boring.

B: I'll take that one straight to the bank.

A: That's it really.

B: But you talk about me.

A: Not really.

B: But sometimes.

A: Sometimes.

B: Ha.

A: It's not a big deal.

B: Course not.

A: More often it's about how fucking desperate you are.

B: Excuse me?

A: Oh come on, I'm kidding.

B: That isn't funny.

A: Take a joke mate.

B: What part of that is a joke?

A: Lighten up would you –

B: – rich coming from the one who fucking begs for sex.

A: I don't beg.

B: You beg.

A: I do not beg.

B: There was that once –

A: – we agreed to never discuss this –

B: – that one time where you were on your knees in front of me –

A: – a change of pace, eh? –

B: – begging me to fuck you. Remember that?

A: It had been a while.

B: For you. You even tried to get me to flip a coin.

A: You did flip the coin –

B: What was it you said? 'Heads we have head.' You don't even like giving head.

A: Says who?

B: Says the girl you wouldn't go down on even after –

A: – I would've done with the coin –

B: What is it you dislike?

A: You haven't got a fire escape hidden in here somewhere?

B: So what is it then?

A: I shouldn't have said anything.

B: What have you got against head?

A: I love head.

B: Could've fooled me.

A: I love getting head.

B: Works both ways.

A: It's a year end bonus, not your monthly salary.

B: This is not a job –

A: – It's beginning to feel like one!

B: But –

A: – Well then, why don't you say anything before?

B: As opposed to?

A: After I've fucked you.

B: Because I shouldn't have to ask. You should want to turn me on. / You should make me want to cum.

A: / How can I do anything if you aren't being honest with me?

B: You've probably never found a woman's clit, much less licked it.

A: Don't be petty.

B: You never even bothered to try to find mine –

A: – and why should I? –

B: Because it turns me / on

A: / I don't care! When will you get it? I do not care. Do I have to spell it out for you? I D-O N-O-T C-A-R-E.

B: You should –

A: Why? Why should I? So you can feel justified in being the whore that you are around me every time I'm bored enough to fuck you? You lap that up. I don't need to convince you.

B: The coin –

A: – it was a coin for God's sake not a legally binding document.

B: Perhaps it should've been.

A: Why do you want head so badly?!

B: Why do you?

A: Better than a fucking Fleshlight.

B: – Is that what I am to you? A sex toy?

A: No, you're better.

B: Oh?

A: Yeah. You clean yourself up.

Silence.

A: Call the fucking landlord would you.

B: I don't need to.

A: Oh for fuck's sake / call the fucking landlord and get over yourself, I don't want to be here and I'm fucking sick and tired of your nonsense, this fucking passive aggressive bullshit

B: /I don't need to call the landlord and don't fucking speak to me that way, you have absolutely no idea and, you are so fucking rude, and – FINE, LEAVE

B *takes out her key and unlocks the door.*

B: Go on then

Silence.

A: You psychopath

Nothing.

A: You locked me in

Nothing.

B: We needed to talk.

A: ABOUT WHAT?!

B: About us.

A: You're delusional.

B: No.

A: You – fucking

B: I'm sorry.

A: You locked me in. You fucking, locked me in…

B: I said I'm sorry –

A: Why? Why did you do it?!

B: You should go.

A: No. You wanted to talk. Let's talk. Go on.

B: I just. I needed to know.

A: Know what?!

B: How you felt.

Silence.

B: I know how stupid it sounds, how fucking pathetic –

A: You put up with all that fucking bullshit about head and sat through all of that – is that how fucked up you are?

B: We needed to talk.

A: Is this what I've done to you?

B: Must be a masochist.

A: You didn't have to lock – *(me in)*

B: Yes I did.

A: No, I would've stayed.

Silence.

B: You should go.

A: You wanted to talk.

B: That was stupid.

A: Talk to me.

B: And say what?

Silence. He waits.

A: Fine. Tell me what it is about head that's so fucking brilliant.

B: Stupid question.

A: That's what triggered this, right? Why does it have to be from me?

B: It doesn't. I'm a sex toy after all. Quick. Easy. Efficient. Clean myself up. Who needs a Fleshlight?

A: You're not a sex toy.

B: You're right. You'd give more attention to a blow up doll. But at least I'm a breathing body and not a corpse.

A: That's disgusting.

B: Are you afraid of not being good? Of me not liking it?

A: That's ridiculous.

B: Then what is it?!

A: It's nothing. It's a time thing.

B: We had time.

A: Well then let's try.

B: Now?

A: Yes.

B: Please leave.

A: I want to give you head.

B: No you don't.

A: Yes.

B: No.

A: It would turn me on.

B: Oh fuck off. You and I both know you don't care about that. It's too intimate for you.

A: Too intimate?

B: You heard me.

A: Fucking piece of work.

B: Either that or you're just so afraid of being shit at it that you don't bother –

A: Fuck off.

B: – but you know, that makes you even more shit at it. Confidence is pretty fucking sexy but you know, I've realized that you just don't have any at all. This is all a show. Pretend to be this bad boy, borderline sex addict, commitmentphobe –

A: You're being a cunt.

B: Oh, am I? I guess I'm just a cunt then.

A: You're better than this.

B: You want a cunt? Nice to meet you.

A: You're so unattractive when you do this –

B: – do what? Speak my mind? –

A: You don't have to play along with our games –

B: This isn't a fucking game! What do you think this is?!

A: Maybe if you told me what you actually fucking wanted –

B: I told you, I told you what I wanted. I wanted head.

A: Come here –

B: – and I'm sick of sucking your cock hoping you'll return the favor –

A: – I'll do it –

B: But instead you always just fucking slip it in because oh, I'm already so wet –

A: You want head? Come here.

B: Fuck off.

A: Seriously, come here.

B: Get away from me.

A: Come here.

B: Why? Why should I let you?

A: I'm trying to make it better.

B: You can't.

A: Shut your fucking mouth –

B: Why? So you can spew more shit at me?

A: I said shut up –

He covers her mouth with his hand.

B: *(Muffled.)* What are /you doing? –

A: / You wanted head. You're getting head.

B *tries to bite him.* **A** *throws* **B** *over his shoulder and onto the bed.* **A** *pins down* **B***'s legs and spreads them apart.* **B** *is not a silent victim –* **B** *is putting up a fight but* **A** *is stronger. This should not be pleasant.*

A: Hold still –

B: – fuck off –

A: – I'm giving you what you want –

A *gets* **B***'s trousers off.* **B** *manages to knee* **A** *in the face.*

A: You bitch!

A *goes to hit her. Stops just in time.*

Silence.

A *gets off the bed.*

He tosses the trousers to **B**.

A: The window is looking pretty good right about now.

B: …

A: Don't be like this.

B: …

A: You're acting like a child.

B: …

A: If I had known you would take it so seriously –

B: – you've got to be kidding me –

A: – sorry you can't take a joke.

B: That wasn't a joke.

Silence.

A: I was doing what you wanted.

Silence.

A: Don't sit there being self-righteous. Don't sit there and pretend that you're the wounded party here. We had a fucking agreement. Clearly you haven't got it in you to keep up your half of the bargain. Fucking tease.

A *goes to leave.*

A: You won't see me again.

B: Good.

A: I mean it.

Silence.

More silence.

It's deafening.

A: You crazy stupid bitch. I can't believe I'm actually going to miss you.

B: You'll live.

He can't leave.

A: One day we'll laugh about this.

Silence.

A: We always do. We will. One day. Promise.

Nothing.

B: Door or window.

He goes.

SCENE 10

Now

B *takes the sheets off her bed.*

Throws the mattress off.

Pulls off the tainted clothes.

Gets dressed.

Redoes her make-up.

It is a ritual of sorts.

Leading to…

SCENE 11

Now

C *knocks at the door, he has wine.*

B: Hey, come on in.

C: For you.

C *reveals a bracelet.*

B: That's gorgeous.

C: It's handmade..

B: Oh?

C: Thought it may be a nice little something. I was thinking of you.

B: You were away a couple of days.

C: A couple of days can feel like a lifetime…

B: Thank you. It's beautiful.

C: You're beautiful.

C *kisses* **B**. *It is still new. This is early days.*

B: Can I get you something to drink?

C: Let's pop this open –

B: – do you not want to chill it?

C: Just bought it, should be fine.

B: Alright.

B *fetches two glasses.*

C: It's funny we say pop it open.

B: Is it?

C: Yeah. Screw top.

C *takes time to pour the glasses. He's very precise. Almost too precise.*

C: To great things happening when you least expect them.

They clink glasses.

B: Cheers.

C: Confession time. The bracelet?

B: You didn't steal it did you?

C: Oh no –

B: Is it an ex girlfriend's? Because that's a bit – *(weird)*

C: My niece stuffed it in my coat pocket.

B: Oh. So this is… a gift from your niece?

C: Don't sound so skeptical.

B: You told your niece about me?

C: Yeah.

B: Sorry. I'm just not used to this.

C: No, I'm sorry. Giving you a bracelet my niece made is probably a bit much for a third date.

B: – No, it's lovely… –

C: God, I blew it, didn't I?

B: No, no of course not.

They drink.

B: How was your day anyway?

C: It was okay thanks. I had to deal with that settlement.

B: How'd it go?

C: Pretty well thanks.

Silence.

B: How was being home?

C: Very homey.

Silence.

B: I wish I lived nearer my mum, you know.

C: Yeah?

B: Yeah. Don't see her nearly as much as I should.

C: How come?

B: Well, you know, work gets so busy – then next thing you know it's been five months and you've been getting by on a diet of WhatsApp.

C: That isn't a thing.

B: What isn't?

C: A diet of WhatsApp.

B: It's an expression.

C: I've never heard it before.

B: Because I've just made it up.

C: Obviously.

B: The idea makes me laugh.

C: Well, it's hard to nourish yourself without genuine substance.

B: Sorry?

C: A diet of WhatsApp. It's all digital. Nothing concrete.

B: Right.

C: You can't hug your phone, or ask it to give you a goodnight kiss.

B: Well you could, you may just look a bit silly.

C: Have you tried?

B: Yeah, Siri told me to get a boyfriend for that.

C: Ah.

B: Sassy little fuck.

C: You swear?

B: You don't?

C: No.

B: Oh, sorry – I hope I didn't offend you.

C: You didn't offend me. Just wasn't expecting it.

B: Because…?

C: You haven't sworn on our dates before.

B: Ah. Must've been on my best behavior. Starting to show my true colours.

C: Next you're going to tell me that you're a serial killer.

B: A serial killer?

C: You know, while you're revealing your true colors.

B: That's a bit of a leap.

C: Sorry, it was a bad joke.

B: Does swearing make you more likely to be a serial killer?

C: I don't know if there are any statistics on that –

B: – It would be an interesting gauge though.

C: Would it?

B: Wouldn't it? Think about it. There's like a ladder of cursing. A chain, maybe? I'll work on the logistics. Or maybe each curse word is associated with a crime, not necessarily murder, that's a bit easier surely.

C: Like, if you say the word bitch you're more likely to shoplift than someone who uses the word witch.

B: Bit tame.

C: But not bad for a first time.

B: Eh.

C: Why, what would you say? If someone used the c-word.

B: Man or woman?

C: What?

B: Is it a man or woman saying it?

C: Man.

B: Well, he's probably more likely to be a misogynistic prick.

C: Than someone who doesn't use it?

B: No, than a man who doesn't use it.

C: Duly noted. Well, I would never say it. *(Beat.)* Can I ask something?

B: I take it I'm not supposed to say, 'you just did'?

C: Right.

B: Go on.

C: It's a bit nosy.

B: Oh?

C: I know I always say you're nosy and I tell you off for it –

B: – starting off really well there –

C: – let me finish.

B: Sorry. Go on.

C: We've been on a few dates now, right?

B: Right…

C: And we've done something really remarkable.

B: Have we?

C: We've gone beyond texting. We've actually spoken. On the phone. On evenings where we had no plans to see each other. I think that's pretty great…

B: Uh-huh…

C: And I know we're waiting – you know, to sleep together. Well, not sleep together, we've done that, but to have sex –

B: – yeah I got what you – *(meant)*

C: – but I think it's been long enough now –

B: – to wait? It hasn't been that long –

C: – no, no not sex. I just think that you are really a remarkable person. Independent, kind, smart. And when I think / of you –

B: / if the next words out of your mouth are 'I want to spend our lives together' we are going / to have some serious issues –

C: / No no it isn't that –

B: – good –

C: – moving a bit quickly there, eh?

B: If you have a point –

C: Would you let me finish?

B: By all means.

C: Hand. Mouth.

She doesn't.

C: If you don't, I will.

She covers her mouth.

C: Thank you. Just until I finish this thought. Okay?

Nothing.

C: Well, I guess... I was going to say... you make me really happy. And... well, I want to know what it is you're after.

She does not move her hand.

C: Unless you'd rather... not...?

She refuses to move her hand until she has been given permission.

C: Any time now...

She doesn't remove it.

C: I promise I'll never make you put your hand over your mouth again if you tell me.

She raises an eyebrow.

C: I just don't want to think this is... you know, a dead end. I'll even tell you first if it makes you feel better.

Nothing.

C: I'm sorry for asking you to put your hand over your mouth. Please speak to me.

C *grabs her hand.* **A** *enters.* **C** *cannot see him.* **B** *can't not see him.*

B: Okay.

C: Ask me.

B: Fine. What is it that you want?

C: I want a relationship.

B: With me?

C: Perhaps.

B: I don't think I remember how to be in a relationship.

C: It's like riding a bike.

B: I'm not sure it – *(works that way)*

C: – there's no rush. Take your time.

B: Thanks.

Silence.

C: I have another nosy question.

B: Nose away.

C: You never said why it didn't work with the last guy.

B: We were never really dating. It was just convenient.

A: If you call locking me in the apartment convenient.

C: You were friends though?

B: Look, we haven't slept together in – oh God, it must be – a year now?

C: Wow.

B: Yeah.

C: Have you seen anyone else since?

B: No. I actually decided to reclaim my virginity.

C: Very funny.

B: The next person I sleep with will be the father of my children. And if you can't accept that, you should go.

Silence.

B: I'm kidding. Relax.

C: I know.

B: Sure about that?

C: Yes.

B: Either I'm a virgin or I sleep around. Which is worse?

C: Virgin.

B: Okay then, stop being so judgemental.

C: I'm not – *(being judgemental)*

B: – could've fooled me.

C: If you want to be a virgin that's your decision and I respect it, although biologically it isn't really possible to actually *be* a virgin again.

B: We haven't slept together, how can you be sure that I'm not?

C: *(He takes a moment too long to respond.)* None of my business.

B: No, go on. What were you going to say?

C: I know you feminists are all about sexual equality and women should be allowed to sleep around but… I don't know. I just don't like the thought of you with someone else.

B: It has nothing to do with you.

C: I know.

B: You're not my boyfriend. And you have no right to come in here and –

C: I know, I know. I'm sorry.

B: This isn't going to work if you're constantly going to be examining my sexual history.

C: I shouldn't have asked. It was none of my business.

B: You're such a solicitor.

C: I'm sorry.

B: Uh-huh. It's fine.

C: Are you seeing anyone else?

B: I have a date tomorrow.

C: Oh?

B: We arranged it weeks ago.

C: How many men are you seeing?

A: Probably zero.

B: That's irrelevant.

C: Of course. Sorry.

B: That okay?

C: I'm confident enough. I'm going to bet on myself.

B: Good. Do that.

The two go silent. It goes on for an uncomfortably long time. **C** *sits on the bed.*

C: Come here.

B: I'm good –

C: Please?

B: Just a second –

C: – come on.

She hesitates before sitting.

C: Closer.

A: Closer.

B: I have some stuff that I need to finish –

C: – in a minute. Come on.

A: Don't push a good guy away.

They cuddle.

A *joins them in bed.*

C: I'm sorry.

B: You didn't do anything wrong.

C: I'm still sorry.

B: Please stop apologising.

C: Okay. Sorry.

A: Christ, man.

C: Look – this is all new. We'll get there.

B: Look –

C: – I know you're scared. Just give this a chance. You just aren't used to this.

B: To what?

C: Being in a relationship. Like you said.

B: This isn't a relationship.

C: It's headed there.

B: But it isn't one.

C: Yet.

B: It may not be one.

C: Look, I told you I didn't mean to offend you –

B: – it isn't that.

C: Do you want to talk about it?

B: Not really.

C: Because we should, you know. Talk through these problems.

A: She's not very good at talking.

B: It's too soon for us to be having problems.

Beat.

B: I want to go to bed.

C: You are in bed.

B: I'm not in bed, I'm on bed.

C: You said you wanted to go to bed, you didn't specify what you wanted to do when you got there.

B: You know what I mean.

C: I know.

B: I can't really sleep when I'm cuddling.

C: Sorry.

B: No, I'm sorry, I don't mean to be in a mood with you.

C: You don't have to apologise.

B: But I am. I'm sorry.

C: It's fine. *(Beat.)* I'm going to sleep at home tonight if that's okay? You're obviously exhausted.

B: Okay.

C: But I'll call you tomorrow so we can organize Monday.

B: Sounds good.

C: Good night.

C *goes to leave.*

B: Hey.

C: Yeah?

B: Could we go dancing on Monday?

C: Sure.

He exits.

A: Salsa?

B: You don't salsa.

A: You could teach me.

SCENE 12

Three years ago

Their first night together.

A *is wearing only boxers. They kiss.*

A: Hey you.

B: Hey yourself.

A: How have we never done this before?

B: Hmm?

A: Gone out. Best first date ever, I think. Probably. Have I told you how much I love that lingerie?

B: Only a dozen times.

A: It's nice.

B: Don't sound so surprised.

A: It's expensive.

B: Well it isn't Primark. We aren't at uni anymore.

A: I like it.

B: Thanks.

A: Tonight's been amazing.

B: Yeah?

A: Yeah. I'm glad the whiskey wore off.

B: Me too.

A: We'll laugh about it one day.

B: Or later tonight.

A: Or now.

B: Or now.

A: Thanks for being so great about it.

B: Magical fingers.

He is a different person. **A** *is attentive, happy, full of energy.*

A: We should've done this years ago. Why did we wait so long to try the sex?!

B: *The* sex?

A: You know what I mean.

B: We'll have to make up for the error of our ways.

A: Absolutely.

B: You know, I used to think you were obnoxious.

A: Me?!

B: Yes, you.

A: I'm a little hurt –

B: You'll live.

A: I'm going to cry myself to sleep now…

B: Oh you poor baby.

A: I need a cuddle to make me feel better.

B: You slick bastard.

B *gets her dressing gown. They cuddle.*

A: I love that dressing gown.

B: You said earlier.

A: And I'll say it again. I love that dressing gown.

B: Just full of love tonight, aren't you?

A: It's a great word.

B: Yeah?

A: I won't use it anymore. No more love.

B: Oh, really now?

A: Yeah. I'll say… appreciate. I appreciate it.

B: Seriously?

A: Or respect it?

B: A given. As you should me and all my choices.

A: Adore it!

B: Adoration is more loving than love.

A: You can't make a word more of another word when the other word embodies the whole definition of the word.

B: Don't be difficult –

A: Any word can mean love if I say it in the right way.

B: Prove it.

A: Pick a word.

B: Car.

A: I car it.

B: You're silly.

A: You're gorgeous.

B: I bet you say that to all the girls.

A: You're the only one I've been with this year.

B: What?

A: You heard right.

B: Really?

A: Yep.

B: That's –

A: – Yeah, a long time, thank you.

B: Why me?

A: There's something different about you. Something special.

Silence.

B: Can I draw on you?

A: Sure.

B *finds a pen.*

A: What's your fantasy?

B: Sorry?

A: It doesn't have to be a sexual fantasy.

B: I don't have one.

A: Everyone has one.

B: I don't, really.

A: You never practised an acceptance speech in the mirror?

B: Only with one hairbrush, but it met its untimely end.

A: Too many speeches.

B: Something like that.

A: You must have something. Okay. I'll go first. So… when I was a kid, there was this village we used to go and visit. Somewhere up north. Can't remember where exactly. But anyway, my mum would take me on these adventures. We'd find an old ruined wall and pretend to have discovered a new civilization, or maybe we'd meet an owl who would tell us about a buried treasure.

B: Did you ever find the treasure?

A: Yeah – it was always in the kitchen.

B: The kitchen?

A: Yeah. Dessert.

B: Cute.

A: So. What's the dream?

B: It's silly.

A: I bet it isn't.

B: It's very simple.

A: The best ones are.

B: I want to be madly in love.

A: Didn't you just break up with someone?

B: Yeah.

A: Did you love him?

B: I mean, he was fine.

A: Oh.

B: It's why we broke up. He wanted to propose and get married and I totally panicked. And all I could think is, god, if my first instinct is complete and utter horror, I probably shouldn't be with him at all.

A: I get it.

B: I know it sounds stupid, and ridiculous, and I can't even believe I'm telling you this –

A: – you can tell me anything. Always.

B: I don't know if I can do it, you know.

A: Have you ever been in love?

B: Once. Felt so bad for my mum when it ended. I cried in her lap for days. She probably wondered what she'd done to deserve listening to me whinge about some stupid guy all the bloody time.

A: Just your mum?

B: Oh, it's a bit weird telling a dad stuff like that really.

A: Are you close?

B: He's not around much.

Silence.

A: We're more alike than you think.

B: Stop it.

A: Seriously. We are. Beyond the family stuff. We both feel like outsiders, we're more intelligent than our peers, we're ruthlessly ambitious –

B: Ruthlessly?

A: Well, ambitious.

B: Better.

A: And we both enjoy each other's company.

B: That I'll agree with.

A: I've missed this.

B: Sex?

A: Intimacy.

B *accidentally hurts him with the drawing.*

A: Ow –

B: – sorry! –

A: It's fine, it's just a cut –

B: Kiss it and make it better?

She does.

A: You're adorable.

B: Go away.

A: I don't think I've never been with a girl quite like you. Quick to smile –

B: – don't get sappy on me –

A: – quick to make things better.

B: It's nice to catch up.

A: We've done more than catch up, surely.

B: Can I ask you something?

A: Shoot.

B: Maybe I shouldn't…

A: You can ask me anything.

She considers.

B: What is this?

A: Whatever you want it to be.

Joy.

SCENE 13

Now

The phone is ringing. **B** *misses the call. She has a voicemail. She listens.*

C: Hi… I just wanted to. Say something. You know, before we go out on Monday. I think that you're gorgeous. You're charismatic. You're intelligent. You're wonderful. I just think that you want something more serious and I'm just not ready for that. I'm sorry to leave this as a voicemail but I think it's better than going dancing and… setting this expectation and then… well, breaking it to you after. I wish you all the best. Really, I do. Anyway… bye.

B *plays it again. Halfway through –* *"Message deleted."*

SCENE 14

Now

B: What is this?

A: Whatever you want it to be.

B *is watching as the assault repeats. She is not physically reliving it herself.*

A *is where he was during the assault. Suddenly, he moves as though he's been kneed in the face.*

A: You bitch!

   The window is looking pretty good right about now.

   Don't be like this.

B: How did we get here?

A: You're acting like a child.

B: I shouldn't have locked you in.

A: If I had known you would take it so seriously –

B: – you've got to be kidding me –

A: – sorry you can't take a joke.

B: That wasn't a joke.

Silence.

A: I was doing what you wanted.

B: That wasn't what I wanted.

   I don't understand how we got here.

A: Don't sit there being self-righteous. Don't sit there and pretend that you're the wounded party here.

B: How we got to the point of actual physical fucking violence.

A: We had a fucking agreement. Clearly you haven't got it in you to keep up your half of the bargain –

B: What happened? You used to have my back.

A: Fucking tease.

A *goes to leave.*

A: You won't see me again.

Rewind.

A: Call the fucking landlord would you.

B *takes out her key and unlocks the door.*

B: Go on then.

Silence.

A: You're a fucking psychopath.

B: I made a mistake.

A: You're delusional.

You – fucking.

B: I'm not a psychopath –

A: You locked me in. You fucking, locked me in…

B: Yes – yes, I did, I'm sorry – please, listen –

A: Why? Why did you do it?! Let's talk. Go on.

B: I just. I needed to know.

A: Know what?!

B: I needed to know – I don't know, it all sounds so pathetic now –

A: You put up with all that fucking bullshit about head and sat through all of that – is that how fucked up you are?

Rewind.

A: I want to give you head. It would turn me on.

B: Oh fuck off.

A: It'll be fun –

B: You never give me head –

A: – I will –

B: – you and I both know you don't care about what I want –

A: Of course I fucking –

B: – you just want a fucking blowjob for the – *(road)*

A: – I've never forced you to do that –

B: – no, no of course not. Just tried to get me to flip a fucking coin until it gave you the answer you wanted. This isn't a fucking game!

A: You want head? Come here.

B: Fuck off.

A: Seriously, come here.

B: Get away from me.

A: Shut your fucking mouth –

B: Why? So you can spew more shit at me?

A: I said *shut up* –

He covers her mouth with his hand.

Rewind.

B: I have a confession.

B *unlocks the door.*

A: You're a fucking psychopath. You locked me in. You fucking, locked me in…

B: I needed to end this – I needed to know once and for all. I didn't think – I didn't… realize, this is what would happen.

A: You put up with all that fucking bullshit about head and sat through all of that – is that how fucked up you are?

B: I didn't deserve this.

A: Is this what I've done to you?

B: You'd give more attention to a blow up doll. But at least I'm a breathing body and not a corpse.

A: That's disgusting.

B: Please go –

A: I want to make this right.

B: I need you to leave –

A: Come here, let me give you head.

B: Not now, I don't –

A: I want to –

B: Please –

A: It'll be great. Relax.

B: I don't want it – please, please let go –

A: Come on, come here

B: Please stop, not like this.

A *grabs* **B**.

B *screams.*

Rewind.

B: … the movie Teeth?

A: What?

B: The one where her vagina has teeth inside –

A: Where do you come up with this shit?

B: Anyway, so it looks like there may be a big promotion coming up, if I nail – *(the next pitch)*

A: Please? Just sex. You don't even have to go down on me. In, out, down. It'll be over in like, two minutes.

B: No.

A: I'm not kidding. Say the word. I'll do it.

B: Fuck off –

A: Let's flip a coin. Heads we have head.

Rewind.

B: Can I ask you something?

A: Shoot.

B: Maybe I shouldn't…

A: You can ask me anything.

B: What is this?

A: Whatever you want it to be.

Fast forward.

The assault beginning.

The hand over the mouth –

Rewind.

A: Whatever you want it to be.

Fast forward.

The hand over the mouth –

The bite –

Rewind.

A: Whatever you want it to be.

Fast forward.

The bite –

Forcing her on the bed –

Rewind.

A: Whatever you want it to be.

Fast forward.

She knees him in the head –

Rewind.

A: Whatever you want it to be.

Fast forward.

A: Bitch!

Rewind

A: Whatever you want it to be.

B: Nothing.

I want nothing.

There is silence.

C: We could've been so happy.

B: I need you to leave.

C: You could've –

B: You dumped me.

C: Only because –

B: – don't you fucking start with me. I was so terrified to give you the chance –

C: – but –

B: – I was terrified to give you the chance and *you* told *me* that you wanted a relationship and you have the fucking gall to turn that around and tell me that *I* want something too serious?

C: Are you listening to yourself?

B: OF COURSE I FUCKING AM

C: We had much bigger issues. We weren't compatible.

B: What does that even mean?

C: I know you feminists are all about sexual equality and women should be allowed to sleep around but... I don't know.

A: And what would your father say, huh? If he saw the little slut he's raised? You think he'd be so fucking proud of you?

C: I just don't like the thought of you with someone else.

B: You know that isn't fair.

A: It's probably why he left, you know. Couldn't bear to see what a fucking disgrace you'd become. Didn't want to hang around to watch you self destruct.

C: It isn't really possible to *be* a virgin again.

B: You know what, you're probably right. I'm just going to be alone for the rest of my life, huh. Because I'm not worth anything.

A: Stop it –

C: It's none of my business.

B: – stop what? You're right. I'm just another whore as far as you're concerned. So fuck off and leave me alone.

B *exits the space. There is silence.*

More silence.

It's deafening. She chooses to step back in.

A:	B:	C:
		It wasn't my intention to hurt you.
Mate.		
	Mate?	
		I was just being honest.
What?		
	You called me mate.	
And?		
		I asked what you wanted.
	Nothing.	
I didn't realize how much you cared.		
		We should talk.
	There's nothing to talk about.	
		About us.
	I don't know what to say.	
		You didn't seem that receptive, to be honest.
I didn't realize I could never fucking get you to leave.		
		Don't get me wrong, I enjoyed our time together.
	Please, don't –	
		I think you're wonderful.
	It's too soon.	
		I'm sorry it ended up this way.
	I don't care –	

I was willing to offer
you everything –

– I don't want –

I can't believe how
much I miss you
sometimes.

- this

You just – you have all
this baggage

I've been seeing this
girl.
Woman, really.

I've been seeing this
girl.

It didn't take long for
you to commit to her,
did it?

Fiona

Madeline.

She just had to bat her
pretty little eyelids at you.

Maybe the bracelet was
a bit much.

Would you fuck off?!

But –

I just don't care, I'm
sorry, I really don't.

I can't believe how
much I miss you
sometimes.

C *exits*

I don't recognise
myself.

I don't know what to
say.

You know what I want?

What I've always
wanted?

Someone.

Someone to fucking
hold at night who will
stroke my fucking hair
and tell me they love
me and that it's okay.

Is that so much to ask?

Is it?

You're the only one
who can bring this out
in me.

I am so, fucking,
furious.

I let it happen.

I want you to feel how
I felt.

Fiona doesn't know.

like everything that
comes after is useless

She can't.

and I want you to feel
what it's like

Ever.

not to want anyone to
touch you

or

She'd leave me.

kiss you

or hold you

I can't look at myself in
the mirror.

you don't deserve that

to be held

you don't deserve love
– you stole it

but –

My joy

You stole my joy.

I didn't do anything
wrong

I hope your fucking
dick falls off.

And your tongue

And your hands –

I hope you look at her

and you look into her eyes

and you see me,

There. Alone.

I didn't mean to hurt
you

And I hope you treat her
with respect.

And human fucking
decency.

And one day,

I didn't mean –

I mean,

One day,

Fuck.

One day I really,

I did. But it was the
moment

Fucking hope,

We did it to each other

with every bone in my body,

I'm so fucking sorry.

that I can forgive you.

I'm so fucking sorry.

Maybe one day.

Not now.

But one day.

Next time –

– There is no next time.

There is no next time.

There is no next time.

There is no –

Blackout. End.

9 781913 630881